ASYLUM

RENEE DANIEL FLAGLER

Printed in the United States of America

First Edition May 2021

10 9 8 7 6 5 4 3 2 1

Library of Congress Cataloguing-in-Publishing Data 2021932547

ISBN 978-1-7347775-6-7

❧ Created with Vellum

Dedicated to all women, especially my Black & Brown sisters.

# Back Then

Back then returns to me
    Like snatches,
    Flickering reels of random recollections
    Worn and gray around the edges,
    Warm and soothing
    Or fiery and fast
    Kindling a pounding in my memory's soul.
    Back then skips time,
    Toddlers spinning like tops
    Falling down dizzy and giddy,
    You show up at my classroom door
    Joy bouncing through my feet.
    I remember your bun
    Smart and neat
    You looked so pretty.
    Back then is sometimes cloudy
    Sometimes clear, like crystal snowflakes
    Fluttering over holiday gatherings
    Gifts piled high spilling over well-tread floors
    Love-inspired pies sitting on sills
    Flavoring the air.
    Dinners served by standards
    "The forks go on the left…
    Knives on the right."
    Back then struggle lacked a conceptual sting.
    Meals stretched across six
    Small ready mouths
    Savored, though sometimes scant,
    Hunger never quite settled

Love looked like food, shelter
And clothes on the back
Crafted by tired
Hands, feet, bodies, minds, hearts.
The sound of it was mute,
The feel, warm.
Back then I skipped by your side
Holding your hand mumbling,
Humming wistful tunes.
Outside by six waiting for his bus,
Running to meet him with wide arms
And an open smile when his burly frame
Rounded the corner.
The quiet hero had come home.
Back then there were fights
I didn't understand,
Tears and shouts
Curses flung and caught by
The thickness of tension
Held in the air.
Other times we all danced to
Tunes from the wooden console,
Wax spinning carefree,
Bodies moving in beats.
He danced with me in his arms.
Back then
That night came.
Blood trickled and hearts cracked
Trusts shattered in lethal shards
Everything changed...forever.
Quiet blackness came after
The cries of the pained.
Lusts betrayed love
Caught it in planted snares

The thickness of angst
Hovered in the blackness
Of the failing evening light.
Hearts hardened
Regrets blossomed
Pride prevailed
And then
We were alone.

n

Was it an emergence or a run?
 Out of muck, Phoenix-like,
 Or a sprint driving far from a flesh
 Wanting so badly to be shed like leprosy.
 Ran so far you became
 Unrecognizable to yourself,
 Twisting and turning like a baby
 Out of the womb still covered in slime.
 Tossed on a people for generations,
 Creating ugliness that shrouded beauty
 And took another 30 years to be unveiled again.
 Look in the mirror every morning and
 Tell yourself you love you.
 A mantra as foreign to the lips as it felt to the heart,
 Any lie becomes believable if you say it enough.
 Who said black was beautiful anyway?
 Lie until it's true to you.
 Little black girl
 With your corn braids spiraled,
 Rounding your scalp like Autobahn curves
 Into a singular sprout
 When naps were pots and pans
 In your kitchen, not a curl pattern.
 Knobby knees black from boyish living,
 Ebony skin silky like espresso before it was
 Suitable for publication.
 Brown bombshell… whaaaaat?
 The stigma of your black skin faded
 But never erased.

Covered implicitly,
Decoded by innuendo.
Brown beauty,
Chocolate
Ebony
Cocoa
Mocha,
Caramel dipped.
Exuding the essence of the earth.
You're pretty for a dark-skinned girl.

TIME PASSED,
Intelligence shrouded the wounds.
Love happened even though you were
No more accepted, just tolerated.
Their validation no longer penetrated enough
To validate you.
Enunciate!
"You speak very well," the white woman said
Examining your tongue with intrigue.
Suddenly you're a caged display
Awing the masses.
You want to beat your chest
and remember your Mama's words
Not in front of them.
That's how the two sides emerged,
Splitting you in two.
Sharp-tongued and loose lipped
Depending on who's in your hearing.
You don't fight the divide.
You perfect the imposter.

The Unlikely Link Between Jim Crow and the Information Age

DID YOU HEAR?
    Hear what?
    There's a Nigger in the White House
    Ruining our country.
    We'll have to take it back.
    How he got there
    Is mysterious at best
    A disastrous atrocity
    Due to traitors on our turf.
    We must get him out
    By any means necessary.
    Gather the troops
    Of true Americans
    From sea to shining sea.
    Each must do their part
    For we've labored too hard
    To make America what it is.
    We stand to lose it all.
    Making things colorful,
    Way too equal
    They'll think they're worthy,
    Forget they're inferior
    And want the same things.
    Next, they'll be CEOs
    All over God's country.
    We must move now,
    Take our country back.
    He'll encourage more
    Make them believe

Anything is possible.
Anything is possible,
Even the president is black.
Doors have opened
From Erie to the Nile.
Rivers were crossed
Swelled to higher ground.
Voices no longer hushed
Despite the ears that ring from our cries.

WE'RE RETURNING to power
Like ancestral kings
Taking back podiums from where
The privileged carved walls and ceilings
In stone
So out of reach that the longest arms couldn't grasp,
Nor could courageous hearts nab
Despite degrees, accolades or tap dancing.
Assimilation could not be attained.
A few slipped through,
Walking through tall fires
Burning all the way to their graves,
Hoping the cracks they made
Could combust into wide flames,
Their sparks reaching children,
Brightening their dreams and
Making tomorrow glimmer hot
Like bright raw suns
This could change everything.
Nothing will be the same
Implement and strike
A take down is in order
From the big house to the hood.

7

Strategy is imperative
Subtleties are key.
Infiltrate the world
Lest they celebrate.
Start with the young
Dethrone future kings
Get the media on board
We'll need their proclivities.
Muddy the language
Old words subtly mean new things
We won't seem racist,
Not that we are anyway.
We're just trying to take back
What has been taken.
That which was rightfully ours.
That which was rightfully ours
Will finally be made accessible

As it should have been so long ago
When our daddies were striving,
Turned down and cast aside,
Stifled by brown and black skin.

*B*ack Then II

WE SAT under the stars
  Between scarred wobbly knees
  Ices dripped blue, white, and red
  Down slim fingers.
  Cornrows twisted down pale scalps,
  Words in jest flew past popping lips.
  Who liked who?
  Who was doing what?
  Chile please!
  Ain't nobody studying him!
  "Him" had small, neat fros
  Too tight shorts and tube socks with
  Colorful bands pulled to the knees.
  Teeth, nose, and ears
  Too large for small brown heads
  Carrying the mismatched look
  Of abstracts by Kandinsky.
  We wore terry cloth rompers
  Jelly shoes that burned under the sun,
  Pig and ponytails that sprouted and laid
  Kinky, curly coils defying gravity.
  Sang
  Chitty Chitty Bang Bang
  And
  Ms. Mary Mack
  Parked hands-on swaying hips
  Bobbed necks to
  Rocking Robin going
  "Tweet, tweet, tweet"

We punched balls down streets
Used sticks for bats
Sought hiders
Tagged, froze, and ran bases.
Laughter erupted as if
Struggles were myths.
Jumped double Dutch
With ropes
Supplied by men
Climbing utility poles.
Cares reside elsewhere.
Mamas stood too long in kitchens
Worn fingers mixing greens with
Love unspoken on sharp tongues,
Caftans over resolves of steel,
Fatigue only revealed in the blood
That pulsed hard through veins.
Work and worry etched in the lines
Of their faces, hardening
Calluses on palms that kept
The young ones in line.
Back then life lived itself,
Both easy and hard.

Grade School

HIS NAME WAS Tim
    That bastard.
    Little black girl
    With braided hair
    Spiraling upward
    Into a singular sprout
    Crushing on boys
    Who didn't see?
    Who wouldn't see?
    Past brown skin.
    Not being enough
    Was never mentioned
    Only confirmed
    Through isolation.
    An occasional "Out of the mouths of babes"
    Revealed the truth,
    Hair too short
    With peas at the nape.
    Skin too dark,
    Color struck
    A legacy of
    Not light enough.
    One day
    She'll learn to love her
    Despite
    Not being validated.

Destined

DANCE WAS in my flesh
  Music in my bones
  Rhythm flowing
  Like blood and marrow.
  Stories curled in my head
  Shared only with
  The figures taped to my walls.
  My adoring crowds.
  I pleased them with
  Eloquent speech
  Elaborate accounts
  Bowed in their presence.
  Shouts of approval
  Through a mouth
  Spewing the sounds
  Of admiration, my own.
  The people
  My audience
  The posters
  On the wall.
  Fast forward
  Published tales
  Resembled reality
  In more ways than one.
  Adoring crowds are now
  Real people
  No longer posters,
  Applause resounds.
  A tongue fluent in inspiration

Gives life to the dreamer,
Stirs belief from the core
Manifest expectations.
Show others their insides
The brilliance that lives there
5 points at a time
Leaving them in awe of themselves.

ℬack Then III

HE WASN'T HOME YET,
    She raged.
    I grabbed the Bible
    Mumbled prayers
    Through clenched teeth
    And blurred tearful vision.
    It was night,
    Far too late.
    He'd been held up by
    Her
    Again.
    She cried enough.
    Anger swept
    The tears behind
    The pain
    Hidden in her heart.
    She grabbed the keys,
    A knife.
    For him?
    Or her perhaps
    Either
    In the car
    She fought with the
    Ignition.
    The engine rumbled.
    So, did she.
    I got in too
    With the Bible.
    She set those angry eyes

On me.
Something shifted.
I refused to get out.
If she was going
I was going with her
To find them
Both.
We drove through the night
Circling blocks and fears
Wallowing in the
Thick, dark, dire muck
Of betrayal.
Because of me
We were back
In the driveway,
Home.
But not him.

Me Too

It happened in adolescence
Right under the noses
Of familial ground.
Seasoned meat sizzling
On the grill,
Smiles all around.
The music of laughter
Jokes and stretched tales
Covered the demands.
Even though some sat
Seconds away on the
Other side of the wall
One hand covers my mouth
Stifling the scream rising
In my tender throat.
Your fingers shoved below my belt
Finding a place to fondle
My innocence into despair.
In minutes it was over.
You went on to party,
Mixed in with the family.
Maybe, I didn't know.
All I could see was
The immediate memory.
While everyone ate
All I could taste
Were tears?
They feasted on soul food
While my soul gnawed on

16

A bitter buffet of rage and fear.
Then, the party was over
At your home
And in me,
But no one would know for years.

Plead on Bleeding Ears

YOU DIDN'T WANT to go but you had to.
There was only one place
You wanted to be, and it wasn't
Where you had to go.
Your pleas were met with
The crack of an iron fist.

*D*em Boys

TODAY WE'RE GOING to write about dreams
    Look into the future and tell me what you see.
    One said:
    "It's bright and I'm in the light
    Not to mention my three-pointer saved the night."
    One said:
    "I'm flying high above the sky
    And someday soon that truth will be mine."
    Yet another:
    "I'm on stage dazzling my fans
    Spitting rhymes, being lauded cause I'm finally the man."
    But You:
    Couldn't seem to write a thing
    A foreign concept for you to dream
    Let me help you, imagine this…
    The one thing you couldn't see was bliss
    What makes you happy or brings you joy?
    "Nothing," you said. "Since I was a little boy."
    "I don't know happy, only pain
    My entire existence has been the bane."
    As my heart folded and finally fell
    In languid little pieces, I felt it melt
    "Violence is something else I know well
    You see, my life is an incarnate hell."
    For the next seven days, here's what you'll do
    Take notice of anything that brings joy to you
    I'm determined to help you make
    Your way to your very own happy place.

You said "I'll try."
And then
You sighed.

$\mathcal{A}$ntonio

I REMEMBER YOU.
In fact, I'll never forget
You changed me
In ways I'd never expect.
At first you held tight
To your heart,
Wouldn't let in the light.
I was there to teach you
But your narrative
Made me see things new.
Teacher became student,
Your life's tale
Made the intelligent prudent.
But the day you asked
That question
Which caused me to gasp,
So simple the words
That seemed
Somewhat absurd.
Do you speak to your sons like this?
Like what?
With words full of encouragement?
Do you think I'm trying to encourage you?
A shrug
A nod
Then "Maybe"
Came through.
Encouragement
To him, was foreign and new.

_D_ilapidated Mind

THE EYE IS STAINED
Seeing reality through depressed-colored lenses.
Joy don't partner with pain
It's rolled over, down for the count
Into a tight ball of blackness
No one can see
While hope runs awry.
A former light dashed
A blinding force that surrenders
To the reign and plight
Of a colorless night.
Happy is a stranger
Living in a foreign land
No relation around these parts,
Only a whispering glimpse
Of a faint whimsy
Through a laugh or moment
That flees and dashes.
"You don't belong here."
The next time it flies by
Capture it
Though it might burn your fingers.
Stash it in a secret place
Till it can no longer be contained
Even if all you know
Is hurt, violence, anger, and pain.

Ally

TOMORROW LOOKS LIKE…
  I pray it looks nothing like today,
  Fear disguised as frustration
  Insolence is a protective wall
  Barely holding years of pain.
  Tomorrow looks like…
  Probably today.
  These walls closing in
  Exhaustion syphoning life
  Playing the same old frame.
  Tomorrow looks like…
  Tomorrow as in the next day?
  Doesn't carry enough hope
  To get through this
  Oppressive wall of angst.
  Tomorrow looks like…
  Metaphorically? Not promising.
  From where my heart sits
  There's hope that a hardening
  Inside will suppress the strain.
  Tomorrow looks like…
  A thousand nights and days
  No bars, dormitories
  Not the pounding sound of
  My father's illicit gait.
  Tomorrow looks like…
  Me facing the silence from
  A lover that let me take the bait
  With a closed mouth

While I live with this stain.
Tomorrow looks like…
Me knowing the difference
Between love and betrayal
Because sometimes from here
It all looks the same.

$\mathcal{C}$onversations with a Black Child I

MY DEAR SONS, they won't see you like I do.
Evident to me is your honor and integrity
Loyal hearts and strong desires
Flames fanned with hopes and dreams
Ambitions set on high.
They don't know you held your
Grandmother's hand as her life slipped away,
Or the tender nuances you shared
Like when you held her face because love
Warmed your fingertips.
They won't even believe that
You kiss your mother every day
Despite being a budding young man
With pubescent friends
Standing steps away.
They'll never hear your infectious laugh
Float through the wood of the floors
Releasing the ease, you can
Only proclaim
Inside these safe familial walls.
But they *WILL* see
The ill-informed nature
Of what they choose to believe,
That those who look like you
Are bound to be:
Gang bangers
Murderous
Beastly
Thieves

Gun-toting
Knife-wielding
Violent
Things
And all the things you're not
Because they refuse to see
Or care to know truth about
Who you were really?
Designed to be.
Know that for them the color of your skin
Will confirm the wrong things
And they'll believe their
Lying bias before seeing
Your possibilities.
So, remember these words
And please stay mute
When they come for you.
Just put up your hands and say,
Please don't shoot.

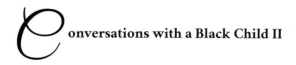

Conversations with a Black Child II

DAUGHTER, you're beautiful
   Despite what they say
   Your crinkly, curly hair
   Is nature's applause
   Your earth-colored skin
   Is of essence and might
   The swell of your hips
   Like the plump of your lips
   And the flavor in your gait
   Or the rhythm of your way
   Is what makes you
   God's masterpiece
   Ephesians 2:10

*L*essons for the Black Son

WORK twice as hard
    I know you're not a thief.
    Get used to being followed
    Through any store with nice things.
    Your character is YOURS
    No matter what they say
    Thug is the new "Nigger"
    They will call you both
    To your face.
    Let the fruit of your anger
    Fuel justice.
    Stand tall
    Even in slander.
    Maintain your pride
    And your word.
    Respect yourself.
    Don't walk around looking
    Like you fit a description.
    Stay away from white girls
    Even if they really like you.
    It will be called rape.

Black Daughter Survival Guide

DON'T POP your gum
    Conjugate your verbs
    Never go out with a scarf on your head
    All you have is your word
    They'll say mean things
    None of them are true
    You *have* to know this
    For yourself.
    They'll assume things
    Don't wear your skirts too short
    Or your weave too long.
    Moisturize your hair every other night.
    Don't worry about proving them wrong
    You can't change their minds
    It won't work anyway.
    Those thoughts are like gorilla glue
    Thick, smelly, unsightly.
    Remember who you are.
    Don't embarrass the family name
    Even if it came from slave masters.

Corporate America

FROM DOMESTIC AND BLUE-COLORED BLOOD. This was unchartered. A ground whose richness I'd never felt under the soul of my feet. I had instincts to walk all these unfamiliar miles, even though catching up with *Your* warped but favored plan was impossible no matter how hard I ran.

I was told I needed more experience. That there were no opportunities for you, Ms. Ambitious Black Girl. Even though… the young blond son fresh out of the frat house who partied with tubs filled with Bud, would soon be my superior, if he wasn't already. He was the son of the executive overseeing human cattle in the building made of glass that overlooked majestic skyscrapers and stately gardens in the center of an overcrowded urban mecca.

So, I took my promotion into my own brown hands. Returned with a well-crafted, excellently coded goodbye. That was met with a scowled smile and poorly veiled eyes that said, "How dare you not let us keep you down?"

eah, I'm Frank.

OF COURSE, your resume opened the door, but perhaps it was your boobs that landed the job. Heh. Years of experience, fresh bubbling ideas and your eagerness to be an 'asset to the company' are all great, but can you just make me a good cup of coffee? I don't care that you studied the science and art of marketing. You're pretty, maybe—and smart enough.

Be like Amy who'll do anything I ask, or like Sara who'll remember my wife's birthday. What about Cindy? See her? She kneels at the altar of me. Your degree has made you much too ornery. Get with the culture of the praise that points toward me. Your ideas are bright. That's cool, but what it accomplishes is disappointing to me. I'm not impressed by the eloquence of your pen. Not when I can't get you to yield to the volume of my masculinity. And why do you get along so well with that *particular* client? Is that a black thing? Though it may fit the business, this is not working for me. I'm going to have to ask you, your master's degree, accolades and qualifications to leave.

When the Time Comes

I WILL NO LONGER HAVE to consider the color of my skin
    First. It won't even matter.
    My credentials will stand out before you realize
    That I didn't grow up in the ghetto
    And there's more just like me.
    Does that excite or scare you?
    My speech won't appear like a phenomenon
    The curves on my body won't make a difference
    You'll accept more than the trendiness of
    My naturally plump lips
    Or the curviness of my hips.
    You'll consider me as I am
    When the time comes, open-ended.
    You won't feel the need to touch my damn hair
    Won't look at my locks like you're visiting a zoo
    Tilting your head in wonderment like
    How did you get it like that?
    You *will* be able to ask me sensible questions
    To help wash away the residue of bias
    Implanted by your parents, by your country.
    My truth won't offend you.
    In fact, it will be as informative as higher ed.
    Until then,
    For now,
    Just let me be a woman.

When the Time Comes II

It will be after all hell breaks loose.
  They say things get worse before getting better
  If that's the case, what could worse
  Possibly look like?
  In worse,
  Is black any blacker?
  Ugly, uglier?
  Brown equal different threats
  Or terror?
  Does bias cut deeper?
  Can the flames of ignorance
  Be fanned any harder?
  Will words tear more souls
  And bigotry be more hailed?
  But then...
  Humans will be human
  Regardless of their hue
  Freedom will be free
  Without lacerating hearts
  The root of pain ejected
  Scars will heal and disappear
  For good and for real

Whisper

Try not to wear your pride
   So loudly
   Careful not to offend
   All that Black Girl Magic,
   Black Girls Rock
   Adds specs to the spectrum
   Why tell the world
   You matter
   When we do too
   Why do you need BET anyway?
   All music matters
   Especially what we exploit, damn
   That hair,
   Big and full of coils and twists,
   Is not meant for the boardroom
   That black too sharp for TV
   And film and books
   And magazines too
   That tongue is too loose
   Or angry and smart
   Where did that come from?
   History is history
   It's in the past, right?
   So what, it's colorless

Token

You're the only one but
    Your tongue speaks the dialect
    Of an entire body of people
    You, alone, are in the room
    With thousands standing
    Behind you, but not
    Work ethic is painted
    With a brush the size of
    A thousand islands
    Brilliant ideas run over
    Slaughtered or ignored, then
    Whitewashed and presented like new
    Competence is met with
    Snarls or even by awe,
    Neither of which are good
    Your place at the table
    Has been tarnished
    With distain,
    Handed over reluctantly
    Since your ancestors
    Were in chains
    The weight of it all
    Pounding you over the head
    Bearing down on your shoulders
    Without choice, you carry it
    Without voice,
    You speak volumes

Wisdom in a Black Box

THEY'LL TALK about you if you do good; *they'll* talk about you if
you do bad Always wear clean underwear
    Clean as you go
    A hard head makes a soft behind
    Don't let your mouth write a check that your ass can't cash
    You ain't gonna pee on me and tell me its rain
    People in hell want ice water
    A closed mouth don't get fed
    It's a poor dog that won't wag its own tail
    Show me your friends and I'll show you who you are
    A shut eye ain't always sleep
    The leaning tree ain't always the first to fall
    You have to feed some people with a long-handled spoon

Ambitions Against the Wall

AT THE TABLE
  You have a place
  as a place holder

Interrogation of the Uncivilized

THE MASSACRE at Rock Springs
  Burning of Black Wall Street
  Sequestering of indigenous bodies
  To a sliver of rock and stone
  So 'kindly'
  Reserved
  Is civil?
  Pillaging the rainbow
  Poisoning descendants
  Of the slain
  With septic white powders
  Boiled into liquid, cooled as rocks
  Carried on ships to rid the race
  Is strategic thinking?
  Desecrating the image
  Of a brown POTUS
  Likening the pecan-skinned
  First lady as parallel
  To a primate
  Tongue wagging grave
  Discredits
  Is just speaking the truth?
  Watering seeds of bigotry
  Fertilizing wastelands
  Of hate-fattened, soul-eating
  Privileged ignorance
  The race is won
  Yet progression is lost?

Swimming openly, naked
In thinly veiled ineptitude
Is okay and quite…
American?

Masculinity of Color

Shaped inaccurate
  Sculpted
  Historical perspectives
  Who is the Black man?
  Stereotypical
  Lacking in depth
  Tired caricatures
  "Thug"
  "baby-daddy"
  "lazy"
  "shiftless"
  Ill-dimensional societal views
  The undercurrent
  The danger?
  This damaging narrative
  Purchased and sold by mainstream
  And also mothers and daughters
  Of the same hue
  Colors perpetuation
  Taints perception
  Justifies treatment
  The muscled media
  Promotes digestible lies
  Black daddies ever evading
  Responsibilities on all sides
  Spreading their *seed* across cities
  So this fosters, confirms and
  Justifies treatment?
  Whose job is it?

To dissect, dispute, discredit
The narrative
The plague of black men.
Our heroes—protagonists
To tell a different story
Than the popular one?
Shine the sun on
Unjustified treatment
A new narrative
Positive perspectives
Combat what has been told
Good black exists
An honorable broad swath of
Images of Black masculinity
Humanized
Unworthy of
Justified treatment
Spotlight the faithful
Fathers and family
At their son's games
And daughter's recitals
Or
Daughter's games
Son's recitals
Call *them* on
Unjustified treatment

White Editor Black Book

BLACK MEN AREN'T capable
    Of love
    Sweet kisses or a
    Gentle touch
    "Can you make these characters white?"
    Black men can't be romantic
    Let alone rich
    They don't believe in love
    Just jungle sex
    Not sweeping women off their feet
    Roses, long walks and dinner
    "I'm *sorry, readers won't relate."*
    Mission: Preserve the narrative

The Dichotomy of Home?

IF IT DOESN'T SOUND like the
    Familiar lilt of unconjugated verbs
    Loose and lazy tongues
    Laid out for soul bending
    Laughter
    Instead of crying from the weary
    Wearing of lead stereotyped cloaks
    Heavy enough to break limbs
    And hopes
    If it ain't unspoken Um mms
    Not spewed through lips but
    Through knowing stoic gazes
    That only the familiar can see
    Through assimilated veils
    That you have to be woke enough
    To spot
    If it ain't a secret society
    Created by the heavy need
    Of being able to see yourself
    Somewhere even when you're
    Never accepted anywhere
    Besides in theory
    By your own or by
    Them
    What is it if you're
    Different enough to be accepted
    By them
    And not accepted enough
    By your own to be perceived

Like less than a sell out
Or told "You talk white"
In a manner that speaks
Neither pride nor shame
Where is it if it leaves you
Straddling the fence between
Who you are and
Who you really are
Or perhaps who you're
Reminded of and should be
According to the crabs
Envious limitations
Or white preservation
Get too much education
Speak too well
And find yourself
Not welcome
Here nor
There
For the most part,
And with all that for which
Blood was shed
And bone crushed
Under the pressure of
Angry waters
You manage to achieve
Accomplish and aspire,
Yet it all
Still leaves you outcast
Questioning your
Belonging.
Then what is home?
Home is nowhere.

*A*nother Token

/TIRED/ of proving just for proof's sake because our hue discredits qualifications upon first sight. That's only if the ethnic clues of our name don't steal the credit first /Tired/ of the surprise fostered by our intelligence because it doesn't match the color of smart. It's not an anomaly. There are more just like me.

Corporate Amerikkka

IT WASN'T me personally that she lacked fondness for
It was the earth brown skin, the audacity of my aptitude
It wasn't me specifically that she wanted to break down
It was the idea that I could...and believed it was so
It was supposed to work—her mastered plan
It had been well laid from the moment I'd been assigned
It worked with the other colored ones
It prompted sharp departures and siphoned incomes
It should have rendered me unwaged
It meant to paint me shiftless and belligerent
It should have been easy to convince everyone
It was how we were..............right?
It was supposed to be her colorless truth over mine
It was supposed to ring true right through the lies
It was supposed to be her doing—my undoing that is
It should have been her satisfaction to break another sis
It was supposed to make her stand taller
It was her version of 'Your Blues Ain't Like Mine.'
It was supposed to make her feel bigger
It wasn't meant to spotlight her lack of interior
It should have pushed me out the door
It should have tattered my will for the possibility of more
It should have sullied my reputation from above
It should have been her singular successful outcome
It shouldn't have been me to have that degree
It shouldn't have been me to accomplish that which she
hadn't
It should have been my detriment to suffer her ultimatum

It shouldn't have been me to have a chance to choose my destiny

It should have been her to say, too bad, now leave

It shouldn't have been me showing leaving wouldn't hinder me

IT SHOULD HAVE BEEN me that allowed her to break me

Whose Truth Hurts More

HELP me understand
  Why my truth offends you,
  Why when I taste reality
  Your mouth stings.
  If I'm bludgeoned
  Should I just bear the pain
  Of a beating unwarranted
  While my bones cry and ache?
  I am wronged as often as you are
  Privileged, but *my* lips should
  Cement the truth even as I
  Choke on my angst.
  Thick black smoke
  Builds in my raw throat
  Yet I should swallow the fire to
  Keep your lungs from turning black.
  Even as I bleed fresh from wounds
  As old as generations,
  Should I disguise my torment
  While my brother lies dead in the street?
  Perhaps devour my rotten verity
  So the offense could let you be.

What I've Earned Off Their Backs

GRANDMOTHERS LAID down
   So I could stand up,
   Lost fingers for reading
   So my story could one day be told,
   Left fresh prints in the dirt
   So I'd know where to go.

$\mathcal{M}$ aking a Black Brother

THAT DAY EVERYTHING CHANGED.
Their blindness made it easy
To inflict all that pain.
They didn't see the student
Who dreamed the unseen,
Studied infinite nights
For the kind of white-coat future
That bloated a parent's chest
With pride-filled swells.
They didn't know
You had parents who cared,
Domestic and blue-collared tired
But willing to stand the rain
To save a son created
Into a tapestry of hope.
It didn't matter to them.
Blue fists busted your lips,
Pounding in torrents
Stinging and hard like hail
Until your eyes bubbled closed,
Dashing more than the light of your sight.
They didn't care that
Depression invited darkness
To cling to your soul for years
Sucking joy like leeches,
Evoking all your fears.
They didn't stick around to see
Your unseen dreams disappear,
Higher ed fade from your grasp

As if someone turned the light
Out on your future.
Yet some consider you lucky
Because
You're still here

*D*ear Mama,

YOU TOLD ME THINGS. Some lay under the foundation of life. Others were for times that came and went. Vital things. Funny things. Nominal things. You taught me things that you never realized were lessons. Or maybe it was me that didn't know because you were the one who was wise with wisdom that expanded like the wings God called you home on. You gave me pearls that matured with my experiences and activated knowledge at hostile times. You told me there would be good days. And bad. Many in between. You showed me life with your living. Lessons learned and pains endured swaddled in one existence with a tapestry of wild colors. From a distance, all I could see was beauty. Only up close did the crimson blood stains come into view. Blues traveled in various hues of depth. Bright sun-like tones of happy swirled between the blackness of life. Colors counted like days in a calendar of years until one day, without my wanting, you were gone.

For everything...thank you.

Your baby,

Renee

ear Daddy,

IT WAS in the last years that I tried hardest to be your daughter. Making up for the time I missed wanting to be a daddy's girl. Indiscretion got in the way. Separation tore us apart. Your soft-spoken nature not wanting to rock the boat. Rage well-managed and covered in cast iron, but when tapped, filtered like lava from lips tight as sciatic nerves. Pain just the same. Loving where you couldn't give of yourself and living where you couldn't love. Regret followed you and then guided you back too late to mend the vacancies gaping from fruit with rotted worm holes.

MY MEMORIES of you were full, then sporadic, and then full again. The middle patched with holidays, graduations, boyfriends, weddings, and encounters like half-eaten meals. We were proud beasts swapping pleasantries. I wanted more. You tried. Then the measure of you was hardly enough for your own living. Age invaded. That was okay. You needed all of you to live. I understood. I was already used to only a part of you anyway. And then the withering began, under our noses. I came to you, felt you leaving. The truth of it lodged in my throat.— would only come out in cries so I wailed while siblings watched, reading the angst on my foreign tongue. The clarity was severe. It was almost over. Death rattled in your chest. You tried to cough it up like phlegm. It refused to rise, going deeper, and spreading its blackness through your cavity until it sucked away your last breath. You were all we had left.

Love always,
Your Precious Baby Girl

South Carolina,

YOU GAVE birth to the transplants of my roots. Ancestral plains running deep across counties. Blood trails covering tears, stifling cries from the human portal of Charleston where I'm pretty sure the fathers of my fathers and mothers of my mother's disembarked before fanning across the deep hellish flatlands of plantations from the Atlantic to the Gulf. The splendor you claim is the same pigment of my pain. My black to your white. The blood of slaves seeps into the soil under a blanket of rich green grass. Bodacious weeping trees thick with branches, beauty, moss, and ghosts. I see the ghosts. Hanging silhouettes of the slain, slumped and rotted like fruit dangling from deadened stems. Naked to the white eye. Majestic homes boast audacious charm and smiling brides as laughter rolls benevolently across acres of spacious plains. Just under the sound of joy is the anguish of a people festering audibly. But you don't hear it. Bubbling over in wailing torment. Old as generations. Loud as tears that bleed through the eyes of their children. I feel them and hear the sounds of their cries in my bones.

Sincerely,
Your Descendant

*D*ear Narrators,

IT TOOK ME A WHILE, but now I realize why your version mattered so much. The narrative you sold sparkled with truth. The sprinkling, light and settling only on the surface, served your perspective and blanched your lies shiny and hopeful. You held the truth's head under water expecting it would die. Instead, it held its breath, preserving the real narrative under a scope. You controlled the chronicling of our shared history, spinning encouraging tales of watered-down triumphs in schoolbooks. Giving black brown children highlights for twenty-eight days of their full lives. It was enough without being too much. They couldn't know the whole story. Couldn't know how deep their strength ran. How many examples of themselves prospered and strategized? That would conflict with the narratives you fed to boys and girls in healthy fattening doses of despair and limitations. You didn't anticipate that we could one day pen our own accounts, take back the narrative and fill in the blanks. You didn't want us to know we were more.

Sincerely,
History's Daughter

$\mathcal{D}$ear Words,

THANK YOU FOR FREEDOM. For becoming a well I can fill with passion. Pack with delight and metaphor. You courted me. I came to love you. You loved me back, expanded right before my eyes. Danced and twirled into enchanted tellings. Living with you on my heart gave light to my years once I no longer denied our connection. I finally committed. You'd been there all along waiting for me to notice that our relationship began way before it began. You had me at "Once Upon a Time". Your rhythm inspires me.

Releases.

Compels.

Consoles.

Comforts.

Sometimes stings, like a good love sometimes should.

Love always,

Your eternal love

*T*hank You Letter,

HAD it not been for you, my skin, tethered from the constant repelling of darts from sharp tongues and predisposition, wouldn't have been so beautifully dense. Romans tells us that knowing that tribulation worketh patience; And patience, experience; and experience, hope. Your battleground has worked my suffering muscle; strength knits my bones; patience is my garment; experience my wellspring; and hope, the promise of my future. So many of us didn't die, we just rose taller. Our heads were bowed, but our backs remained straight. I thank you for revealing the conqueror in me. My blood pumps renewal, recovers from offense before contamination could even set in. Resilience is indelible in my DNA, passed down from generations before to my children's children, and the children to come. You've made us a people of impeccably polished vigor. Though that wasn't your intent.

Warmest regards,

A Warrior

_a_ sylum

WHOSE TRUTH IS TRUE?
The telling of truths
A sanctuary for the
Sanctity of realities
Or dumpster for
Prickling insanities.
Depends on who's
Listening
…shhh
To the consciousness
Of a collective story
Recounted by one.
Here lie the bones
Emptied by a people
Of singular sight
Not wanting to see
Their reflection in
Another's dwelling.
Life made complex
With living even as it
May be grueling,
Worth the climb
On back and shoulders
Whether for progression
Or
Oppression.

n Ten Lines

CAN A WHOLE EXISTENCE BE SUMMARIZED?
    Birthed into hopes, flickering lights through time
    Milk fattened and readied for shearing like lambs
    By the sharpness of the oppressor's cutting lips.
    Clothed in armor to block darts of insolence
    Though innocent of offense but still blamed,
    Taught to wade through threats imbedded in DNA.
    Growth steeped in resilience where survival reigns,
    The hotter the water the more you can handle angst
    Makes adversarial living as subtle as the American Dream.

Black White Girl I

Conjugated verbs
Flowing from
Dark lips
Unspoiled diction
Articulated easily
In verse
Well-spoken
Expressed via
Knitted tongue
Unmitigated desire
Burgeoning from
Curious wonder
Adventurous spirit
Stemming from
Uncharted ambitions
Well read
Quoting adages
Of scholars
Made them
Call me
"White Girl"

Black White Girl II

"DOES YOUR SISTER *STILL* ACT WHITE?"
    Her statement met with eyes
    Flashing in shades of rage
    Contained by the confines
    Of a shared workplace.
    But she'd been here before;
    Different person with
    The exact same flaws.

Quoting Audacity

You GONNA LET me hit that?
   How come they picked you?
   Momma, she's dirty
   (*Says the little white boy in the*
   supermarket while
   his momma pretends not to see
   his little hand pointing up at me)
   I'd rather hire a man
   You know they're not educated
   those blacks and Spanish
   Show me homes in Astoria
   just not near black people
   There are no opportunities
   For promotions at this time
   (*Never mind the blond boy's*
   new position since he's the son
   of an executive)
   You sound white on the phone.
   The most interesting thing…
   I was to eat each
   Declaration without
   Ever once
   gagging.

*D*ear Change,

IF YOU COULD JUST MOVE FASTER—PERHAPS, just perhaps...the child I bore in the sheer hope of a changed world could maneuver unscathed. Perhaps teachers wouldn't label her sassy just because she is smart. Intelligence lasts longer anyway. Maybe she could be rightfully upset and voice her discontent without the stifling weight of an angry black female brand sizzling her manner. Maybe she won't choke from the thick noxious scent of her own burning brown skin. If you could hurry, you'll be just in time for her to be viewed as the bright young woman she's meant to be instead of a budding ghetto fabulous diva like some enjoy believing—even though she never lived a single day in the ghetto. They won't watch her, waiting for something ignorant to fall from her full lips so they can prove themselves right in their own minds. Possibly, her perfected speech could be appreciated, not doubted, cast as an anomaly. Her tongue stared upon as if she spewed ancient languages and not the Queen's English.

Sincerely,
Desperately Hopeful

*D*ear God,

YOU SAID we should *rejoice in hope* and be *patient in tribulation*. If patience builds character and rejoicing glorifies You, is there exuberant glorification in Zion for the mothers of brown and black slain sons? *Weeping endures for a night, but joy comes in the morning.* Will the light of that morning sun stretch over a life etched in wretched nights? You said we are more than conquerors, but we seem to always be the conquered. Help me understand because it appears to be different—the lighter the skin, the easier the win. I don't question *You*.

I just have so many questions.

Yours in truth,

Your Child

Dear Prayers,

PLEASE, allow me to beseech you. My son's life depends on your answer. Morning after morning, I implore that when he leaves for school or work or just to hang, an attempt to make himself a better man, to build his heart and mind, to gain that which can't be beaten away, that he will make it back home to us. Safe. Whole. Alive.

I know I ask repeatedly, but every day offers a new feast of aggressions. You see, he drives a car. It's not fancy, but he worked tirelessly and saved until change boasted itself into dollars sure enough for four wheels and coverage to mend accidental breaks. A vehicle he calls his own and paid for by the very sweat of his back, not by entitlements. It's not luxurious, but simple. Four doors. Gray. Compact. But unassuming or not, he needs only to bear black or brown skin behind the wheel for a simple broken brake light, probable cause or simply nothing at all to lead him to being carried by six and buried just as deep. Like so many bodies made infamous by hashtags. Broken. Defamed. Deceased.

Prayers, if you will, don't mind the insistence of my words. Just grant my dire requests. You see, he has a future imagined as bright and bustling as the shooting stars. There's a corner office waiting patiently to bear his name. There's a passport eager to be stamped while he tries the languages and foods of foreign lands on his tongue. Great walls and towers await his awe. A wife and four adorable children look forward to calling him Honey and Daddy. This was his declaration. Two boys and two girls. The boys must come first to protect their little sisters. His future knees yearn for the sitting of his babies, wanting to be read their favorite stories that were once read to him. *Run, run as fast as you can.* He'll introduce *The Gingerbread Man* with the same nostalgic admiration that makes his eyes gleam at the fair age of nineteen. He can't wait to live. Long. Bold. Free.

If you will continue to consider my pleas, I know he will survive. Tomorrow will greet him, bubbling with possibilities. Snatch him by the heart. Float on ambition. Press with perseverance. And dine on the pride of accomplishments, fueling success he couldn't fathom decades before. So, when the sun rises again, I'll be there to ask once more and once more again with the lighting of every new day afforded to my own eyes. Even if I lose my sight, I'll plead through the darkness. I'm afraid that if I don't, he just may not make it home. Alive.

Desperately submitted,
Black Mother

Dear Daughter,

I'M TRYING DESPERATELY NOT to fail you. To prepare you for the sting of the life you're destined to live. The cushion in which you're guarded will be stripped away. Not by my hands, but by the world. If it were up to me, I'd never release you to the dreadful veracity of life, but I must. I wish I could cover you under the safety of my wings forever or equip you with a remedy for all you're fated to face. You're becoming a woman— beautiful and strong, yet graceful. And the problem is that you're becoming—a woman. And not just a woman, but a black woman.

A Black. Woman.

Your #MeToo awaits you. Ready to chip away at securities put in place by the doting of Daddy and me. All I can say is that when it happens, use your voice. Don't be browbeaten and receive your brokenness with open arms. Fight for your soul. Dance in your healing.

Prepare for the expectancy that your irritation, even justified, will be a cultural misstep, indelible on your DNA. You'll have to direct it like a cast of characters starring on stage because *they* will certainly watch, looking forward to the blunders and the climax just the same and blame you for both offenses and your reaction.

They'll try to suppress your voice. Make your ideas appear absurd coming from your tender tongue, recycle your words under the guise of masculinity and spew the fresh theories like they'd pondered them themselves with a level of brilliance unforeseen. And their world will receive it with celebration.

Ground your heels into the space you occupy. It's yours and you deserve to stand there no matter what they may say. Some will attempt to push you out of it, believing you are not worthy. Others will bribe you for it, but it's impossible to steal a destiny that's rightfully tethered to your spirit. So stand in it and don't worry. Your skin will heal tougher when the darts stop burning.

Faithfully,

Your mother

Can I Just Be a Woman?

Not angry
    Not black
    Not angry and black
    Not a nag
    Not a bitch
    Not thin
    Or too fat for that dress
    Not insecure
    Not standardized
    Not caring if my babies left me with a pouch
    Not just having a nice rack
    Not objectified
    Not sexualized
    Not victimized
    Not heckled
    Not a prude when not in the mood
    Not a slut because I enjoy sex
    Not whorish in my fitted wears
    Not fondled
    Not having 'asked for it'
    Not being able to say, Me Too
    Not incapable
    Not always being carried
    Not never being carried
    Not diminished
    Not excluded
    Not disrespected
    Not cast aside

Not overly sensitive
Not intimidated
Not being told this job is more suited for men
Not needing to be superwoman

*A*sylum II

A PLACE WHERE...
>   There's sanctity of sanity
>   Even when challenged.
>   Most deem its walls fit
>   For the mentally imbalanced.
>   There is illusion in stability
>   And mindfulness
>   For the shifts are too certain
>   Too sharp, too deep.
>   Most credit you as
>   A holding cell, good use
>   for the troubled, but what I see
>   Are warm hues of refuge.
>   Sacred thoughts are housed
>   Angry energies reside
>   A respite for shouting at
>   All that's unjust and denied.
>   There is sanctuary.
>   Truths untainted remain alive
>   Narratives aren't ill colored
>   Highlighting legacies of lies.
>   Realities can be preserved
>   Giving certainties a sacred home
>   Not perfect though,
>   Some broken things and bones.
>   Recovery is evident
>   Not clouded with thieves
>   Righteous intolerance for
>   Opposing beliefs.

Honesty doesn't yield a rainbow
And reality sometimes seems
Darker than the blackest night
Still, saneness is redeemed.
Truth stands tall
Even if beaten,
Tired of the bout
For genuine reflection.
All can be what it needs to be
Without need of defense
Hurt, agony, struggle, grief
Tears spilling years of angst
Like a grandmother's bosom
Where aches can subside
Since the pressure can seep
Through watering eyes.
There's nothing to hide
No need to explain
The raw beauty of living
Through the ugliness of pain.
Safety lives as a pulsating
Right, visceral and naked
Perhaps even unshaven
Though accepting and unwavering.
There's rest for my weary portion.

In the Thick of It

YOU PULL into your driveway
    On a day that extended
    Far too long
    And can't seem to turn off
    The engine that Swells and revs just like
    Your heart.
    Your hand on the key
    Does not turn.
    Instead, you're pulled back
    Into the thick of the day
    When the heat was the highest
    In the midst of brisk winter air
    And remember how hard you
    Tried.
    How you grinned in the face
    Of rejection piled high,
    Swallowed the insecurities
    Cutting off your air,
    Swatted micro-aggressions
    With your mental sword,
    Sought might in the
    Crevices of your being
    Hoping to surely find
    Enough to carry you
    Home.
    Your mind is back in the car
    Finally, you shut off the engine.
    It's over…again
    Another day but not your situation

And while you're alone
You take that chance
To try and breathe
And let it all go
But can't find breath enough
To release all the despair.
Instead, the burden thickens
In your throat, clogging.
Internally you moisten.
Water floods your being
Starting from your toe tips

REACHING your belly
Making worry take flight.
It rises to your head
Fills it and spills through
Your eyes.
You must finish crying
Before you get out of the car.
Wipe your face
Settle your heave
Find a smile
Paste it on
Gather strength from past wins
Extract the key
Push open the door
Walk the path to home
Home is supposed to be
Your sanctuary but it
Reminds you of all
You need and
Why it all matters.
Continue toward the door.

Move forward
Walk the green mile
Step into your home
Pretend to be happy
Kiss your husband
Hug your kids.

My Dear Abby

WE MET on a mission to bring women together. White, black, brown, red. We had hearts and resolve in common. Two women wanting to see society shift the paradigm. Not women's rights, but equal rights. Together with the others, we were going to bring down the mantle with unity. Standing shoulder to shoulder, breasts lifted, beating them like beasts if needed. A war cry rising in our parched throats. Ready to march toward the sun. Fresh horizons. We spoke the truth in each other's presence without offense. I had no white friends at my backyard BBQ. You had no black ones but wanted to right our existences to match the fight in us. You and your Jewish humor and me with my black sass. Somehow, we stepped into refuge like quicksand. You wanted me to be your black friend. A place where you could explore authenticity. You tried this in other places but got burned. Asked me where you went wrong. There was no redemption there. As proud as I am to be black, a descendant of slaves made from steely resilience. There are some of us that are too black for everyone's good. That's the thicket that you and your friendly, advocating, good, white, Jewish intentions stepped into. And it could only choke you. Just like the indelible bigotry to which Obama's mere presence was an offense, threatening their America. Where privilege is not acknowledged but embraced. It's capable of siphoning the life from us all. Be careful where you step.

Sincerely,

Your Black Friend

Revelation

MAYBE SOON IT will all change
   Black sons seen as boys
   Not monsters and violent men
   Not thugs and obviously part of
   Gangs
   Not violent felons
   Before arraignment
   Not profiled without
   Complaint
   Maybe finally black girls can live
   Without being stripped of innocence
   Not having to be seen as a girl before
   Race
   Not being judged for wearing braids
   Not having to code their colorful ways
   Not growing into women whose
   Beauty isn't embraced
   Not considered angry when
   Fighting for their
   Place
   Maybe soon it will all be different
   Women and girls valued for worth
   Not having to live and work for less
   Not having to prove their whole intent
   And being offered their fair chance
   Not objects wrongly meant
   For misogynist pittance
   But recognized for
   Brilliance

Maybe more progress is being made
Where marginalized and outliers
Are having their day
Where people are listening
And there's truly some change
Where voices are rising
And oppressions are weighed
For their true impact
And prices are being paid
And justice will no longer
Be delayed
Where hope remains

Asylum

THIS BOOK of poetry is a personal institution erected to serve as a sanctuary for the experiences, thoughts, and ideas of a 21st-century black woman—a visceral collection of reflections about race, bias, injustice and hopes; the telling of autobiographical experiences of a singular black woman, mother, and a professional; a safe haven for the joys and pains of being an African American and a woman in America. The reflections are steeped in historical contexts that penetrate the present and shape the future. It is a resting place for unsettled sentiments, anger, prayers, and pleadings against the backdrop of a society divided. Its hope is to display the insides of black and brown lives to knit cultures, races, men, and women together into a tapestry of understanding. Asylum is one poet's safe place where the sanctity of her truths may find refuge.

ACKNOWLEDGMENTS

To God be the glory! To everyone else, thank you for receiving me as I am and as I evolve.

ABOUT THE AUTHOR

Renee Daniel Flagler is an award-winning writer, coach, adjunct professor and speaker who is passionate about inspiring women and youth to pursue their passion and purpose. Renee is the author of several books and she also writes romance novels under the pen name, Nicki Night. Her poetry has appeared in *Ink & Voices.* Renee received an MFA in Creative Writing from The College of New Rochelle and was the recipient of the graduate program's inaugural Creative Writing Division Award for Excellence in Writing and Commitment to the Profession. She is an advocate for empowering youth in the United States and abroad. Connect with Renee through social media on Facebook, Instagram, LinkedIn or Twitter and visit Renee at ReneeDaniel-Flagler.com.

Made in the USA
Monee, IL
23 May 2022

96919934R00050